Pink Nails

by Dawn McMillan
illustrated by Gregory Baldwin

Someone is coming.
Run home, wombats!
Run fast!
Here comes a human!

Slip!
Crash!
Bash!
Smash!

"I can see a hairy nose.
A big, hairy nose!" said the human.

"I can see a hairy nose.
A very hairy nose!" said the wombat.

"I can see a very scary, hairy nose.
And some very *big*, scary teeth!"
said the human.

DONOTREMOVE

"I can see a very scary,
hairy nose.
And lots of scary *little* teeth!"
said the wombat.

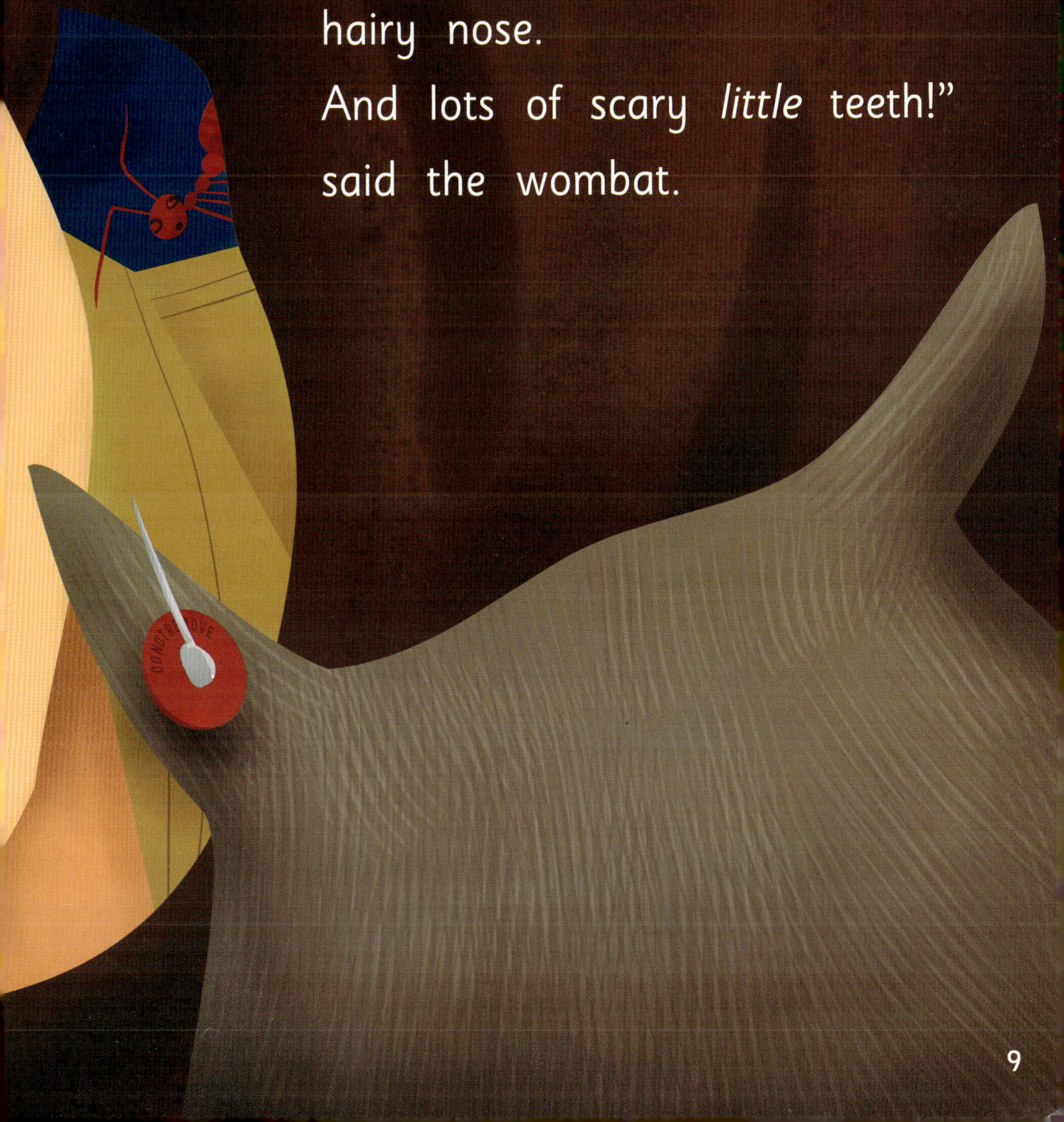

RANGER

"I can see very scary nails.
Long, pink nails!" said the wombat.

“The long, pink nails are digging in my burrow!” said the wombat.

DO NOT REMOVE
ANG

"Hey! Now the long, pink nails are coming closer and closer! They're coming after me!" said the wombat.

“But they are not going to get me this time!” he shouted.